ID0926507

The Name of Love

THE NAME

Classic Gay Love Poems

OF LOVE

Edited by
Michael Lassell

A Stonewall Inn Book
St. Martin's Press / New York

The editor and the publisher are grateful for permission to reprint the copy-
righted poems in this anthology. Permissions appear on pages 80–83, which
constitute a continuation of this copyright page.

Design by Jaye Zimet

Library of Congress Cataloging-in-Publication Data

The name of love : great gay love poems / Michael Lassell, editor.
    p.   cm.
  ISBN 0-312-11863-5
  1. Love poetry.   2. Gay men's writings.   I. Lassell, Michael, 1947–   .
PN6110.L6N36   1995   94-36026
808.81'9354—dc20   CIP

First Edition: February 1995

10 9 8 7 6 5 4 3 2 1

This book is dedicated to
Assotto Saint
(1957–1994)
for his love of poetry
and of poets

SPECIAL THANKS
For services rendered:
John Gill, Richard Labonte, Carl Morse,
Robert Rimmer, Ira Silverberg

For blazing trails:
Stephen Coote, Ian Young

IN MEMORIAM
Walta Borawski, Tim Dlugos, Roy Gonsalves,
Bo Huston, James Carroll Pickett,
John Preston, Craig A. Reynolds, George Stambolian,
and
Bob "Sonny" Cushman, Michael "Max" Roberts,
Peter Mark Schifter, Franklyn Seales,
Jim Tudor, Danny Warner

T h e   N a m e   o f   L o v e

SONNET 29

When in disgrace with Fortune and men's eyes,
I all alone beweep my outcast state,
And trouble deaf heaven with my bootless cries,
And look upon myself and curse my fate,
Wishing me like to one more rich in hope,
Featured like him, like him with friends possessed,
Desiring this man's art and that man's scope,
With what I most enjoy contented least—
Yet in these thoughts myself almost despising,
Haply I think on thee, and then my state,
Like to the lark at break of day arising
From sullen earth, sings hymns at heaven's gate.
    For thy sweet love remembered such wealth
      brings
    That then I scorn to change my state with
      kings.

TRYING TO WRITE A LOVE POEM

For Michael Bronski

Since most of my words go to describe
loves that fail, tricks who come & go,
it's no surprise I have no poems for you.

Shall I, trying to write one, say: You
are the man who stole white lilacs from
Harvard to help me find spring in a

dull season? Or that three years ago we
met in a bath house in New York City, strangers
making love in the shelter of sauna & steam?

Would it be too silly to say I like to think
we're Leonard & Virginia Woolf? Don't worry—
I'll not tell which of us is Virginia. But

if I suffer a total breakdown after trying
to write you this poem—& if you
drop all work on your next essay to

put me together, take care of my cat, they'll
know. Meanwhile, *you* should know that
when I see aged couples clutching each

other, walking quick as they can from
muggers & death—I see us. & that if you
die first, someone will have to, like they

would a cat without hope or home, put me to,
as it's sometimes called, sleep; & though you
don't believe in heaven, & taught me how empty

& odd my own plan for it was, I imagine we've
already known it—at the baths, in your
loft bed; in stolen lilacs, in each stroke you

give my cat, my cock; & though I'm agnostic
now, I never question why the archangel who
sent down the devil is called Saint Michael.

THE FIRST KISS

at first
a feeling like
silk, then
a slight motion
of lip on lip
and breathing.
I take your
lower lip
into my mouth,
delight
in its blood-round
softness, re-
lease it. we kiss.
your tongue
explores; for
the first time
it touches mine:
tip and surface,
root and vein.
our eyes open.

SHOULD IT BE GIVEN ME
(NO. 48)

Should it be given me
constantly to kiss
your lovely eyes, Iuventius,
until I've kissed too many times
to count,
I still would deem it
not enough:
not if more closely packed
than rows of ripening corn
the harvest of kisses
I gather.

TRANSLATED BY EUGENE O'CONNOR

WHEN I HEARD AT THE CLOSE
OF THE DAY

When I heard at the close of the day how my name
    had been receiv'd with plaudits in the capitol,
    still it was not a happy night for me that
    follow'd,
And else when I carous'd, or when my plans were
    accomplish'd, still I was not happy,
But the day when I rose at dawn from the bed of
    perfect health, refresh'd, singing, inhaling the
    ripe breath of autumn,
When I saw the full moon in the west grow pale and
    disappear in the morning light,
When I wander'd alone over the beach, and undress-
    ing bathed, laughing with the cool waters, and
    saw the sun rise,
And when I thought how my dear friend my lover
    was on his way coming, O then I was happy,
O then each breath tasted sweeter, and all that day
    my food nourish'd me more, and the beautiful
    day pass'd well,
And the next came with equal joy, and with the next
    at evening came my friend,
And that night while all was still I heard the waters
    roll slowly continually up the shores,

I heard the hissing rustle of the liquid and sands as
    directed to me whispering to congratulate me,
For the one I love most lay sleeping by me under the
    same cover in the cool night,
In the stillness in the autumn moonbeams his face
    was inclined toward me,
And his arm lay lightly around my breast—and that
    night I was happy.

INDIAN SUMMER

That summer, Charlie drew a cunt
with a black crayon, taught me
how to lick the alphabet.
My mother almost caught us
in her drawers, putting on
the panties and gowns. He slept
in my bed every night after
his parents split. He taught me
how to trust my pouty lips
wrapped around his hairless cock,
tongue sliding across his crack
the way I sealed my letters home
while away at camp. That summer
we rode each other like horses,
fearing Indians in the bushes
along the edge of a bluff.
Then it was over. We cried
at the airport. He promised me
postcards from another world.
When school started again,
I wanted to show him all
the stamps that I had mounted.

FROM THE HEALING
NOTEBOOKS
(NO. 9)

During the night you disappear
beneath the blankets. I feel you

wet between my legs. I hold
your head in both my hands.

You come up for air. I smell
myself when you kiss me.

Do you remember the first time
undressing in your parents' house?

Do you remember calling me from the bar
telling me you had to see me again?

Do you remember how scared we were?

FIRST SEX

This isn't it.
I thought it would be
like having a boned pillow.

I saw myself turning
over and over in lust
like sheets in a dryer.

My style was reckless,
wool dry. Other than mine
there were little or no arms.

I could whisper anything
into an implied ear
and praise would rise
like a colorless, scentless gas.
Then I would breathe to sleep.

But my lover moves.
And my lips grow numb as rubber
before I capture half the ass
that rose like Atlantis
from my dreams.

I try to get his shoulder blade between my teeth.
He complains, pillow in his mouth.
Doesn't mean it.
Means it.

He rolls onto his back,
face raw and wet as fat,
like it has been shaken from nightmares.
I don't know how to please this face.

Tomorrow when he has made breakfast
and gone, I will sweep
the mound of porno from my closet,
put a match to its lies.

I will wait in my bed
as I did before, a thought ajar,
and sex will slip into my room
like a white tiger.

THE POET TO TELESPHORUS
(11.26)

O my succor, darling boy,
Telesphorus, whose like I never held
in my embrace before:

Give me kisses sweet and moist
with vintage wine, let me quaff the cups
half-emptied by your lips.

Grant me then love's joy unfeigned,
I'll say: "No finer drink served Ganymede
to slake the thirst of Jove."

TRANSLATED BY EUGENE O'CONNOR

LOVE DOESN'T EXIST

love
doesn't exist
you tell me

it's a lie
that there are
lovers

the pure
invention
of fools

you explain
concealing
your surprise

as you notice
in the window
of the café

both of our
shadows
embracing

SONNET 8

Sometimes I wish that I his pillow were,
  So might I steale a kisse, and yet not seene,
  So might I gaze upon his sleeping eine,
Although I did it with a panting feare:
But when I well consider how vaine my wish is,
  Ah foolish Bees (thinke I) that doe not sucke
  His lips for hony; but poore flowers doe plucke
Which have no sweet in them: when his sole kisses,
Are able to revive a dying soule.
  Kisse him, but sting him not, for if you doe,
  His angry voice your flying will pursue:
But when they heare his tongue, what can controule,
  Their back-returne? for then they plaine may see,
  How hony-combs from his lips dropping bee.

FROM A SHROPSHIRE LAD
(NO. XV)

Look not in my eyes, for fear
   They mirror true the sight I see,
And there you find your face too clear
   And love it and be lost like me.
One the long nights through must lie
   Spent in star-defeated sighs,
But why should you as well as I
   Perish? gaze not in my eyes.

A Grecian lad, as I hear tell,
   One that many loved in vain,
Looked into a forest well
   And never looked away again.
There, when the turf in springtime flowers,
   With downward eye and gazes sad,
Stands amid the glancing showers
   A jonquil, not a Grecian lad.

THE HILL

We walk together this evening,
arm about shoulder, arm about waist
not knowing what is mine,
Now—so much has passed,
boundaries blurr'd, grown faint or faded blue,
the life beneath—a jewelled toytown—
beneath the lane that leads us to heaven
where stars are leaping Bengal cats
and your eyes a firmament of Truth.

You murmur mutely how you'll enter me again
to scatter moons inside my yielding frame
a milky way to ornament my soul,
to still the drone of other lives
so we may mount our hill
Intact.

Two faces, made sad by brittle beauty
Twin heads of the Caesar on an ancient coin
Now, of infinite worth,
Now—ten years from now.

WHAT'S IN YOUR MIND, MY DOVE

What's in your mind, my dove, my coney;
Do thoughts grow like feathers, the dead end of life;
Is it making of love or counting of money,
Or raid on the jewels, the plans of a thief?

Open your eyes, my dearest dallier;
Let hunt with your hands for escaping me;
Go through the motions of exploring the familiar;
Stand on the brink of the warm white day.

Rise with the wind, my great big serpent;
Silence the birds and darken the air;
Change me with terror, alive in a moment;
Strike for the heart and have me there.

FROM THE LAST ROMANTIC

when I talk to him, I keep spitting flowers. they strike him and immediately melt like huge snowflakes. hitting his eyes they turn into fringed poppies but are gone in a blink. they hit his mouth, his chest, his thighs. as they expire they make tiny sighs like honeybees so burdened with pollen they can't lift themselves from the flower. of course, he acts loutish while this is happening. he grimaces as if to say "look what I have to put up with!" he goes blank. he yawns. and the snowflowers come thick and fast. they are so many, finally, they stick all over him. little drifts in the folds of his elbows. more in his lap. it piles up on his shoulders. covers his head like a cap. clogs his mouth—he never says much to me anyway. his gestures freeze. his body becomes an outline. and, at last, his eyes—our one point of contact that tells me he is bruised by my love as I am bruised—his eyes dim and go. oh, come back. I promise to stop talking. I'll go away. only come back. covered in flowers. look at me. say it with your sullen eyes.

MIRACLE

If time holds a miracle
we'll dance together
as two old men:
sunstroke scalps
dropped buttocks, watery thighs.
But our hands
how our bony, veiny, trembling hands
will find their partners
palm to palm, fingers rung round each other
and hold on tight
tight.
Dance me
dance me across the floor.
I'll stay with you
if time holds a miracle.

TO P.O.

The whitewashed room, roof
of a third-rate Mohammedan hotel,
two beds, blurred fan
whirling over yr brown guitar,
knapsack open on floor, towel
hanging from chair, Orange Crush,
brown paper manuscript packages,
Tibetan tankas, Gandhi pajamas,
Ramakrishna *Gospel,* bright umbrella
a mess on a rickety wooden stand,
the yellow wall-bulb lights up
this scene Calcutta for the thirtieth night—
Come in the green door, long Western gold
hair plastered down your shoulders
from shower: "Did we take our pills
this week for malaria?" Happy birthday
dear Peter, your 29th year.

BLACK BEANS

Times are lean,
Pretty Baby,
the beans are burnt
to the bottom
of the battered pot.
Let's make fierce love
on the overstuffed,
hand-me-down sofa.
We can burn it up, too.
Our hungers
will evaporate like—money.
I smell your lust,
not the pot burnt black
with tonight's meager meal.
So we can't buy flowers
for our table.
Our kisses are petals,
our tongues caress the bloom.
Who dares to tell us
we are poor and powerless?
We keep treasure
any king would count as dear.
Come on, Pretty Baby.
Our souls can't be crushed
like cats crossing streets too soon.

Let the beans burn all night long.
Our chipped water glasses are filled
with wine from our loving.
And the burnt black beans—
caviar.

EPISODE OF HANDS

The unexpected interest made him flush.
Suddenly he seemed to forget the pain,—
Consented,—and held out
One finger from the others.

The gash was bleeding, and a shaft of sun
That glittered in and out among the wheels,
Fell lightly, warmly, down into the wound.

And as the fingers of the factory owner's son,
That knew a grip for books and tennis
As well as one for iron and leather,—
As his taut, spare fingers wound the gauze
Around the thick bed of the wound,
His own hands seemed to him
Like wings of butterflies
Flickering in sunlight over summer fields.

The knots and notches,—many in the wide
Deep hand that lay in his,—seemed beautiful.
They were like the marks of wild ponies' play,—
Bunches of new green breaking a hard turf.

And factory sounds and factory thoughts
Were banished from him by that larger, quieter hand
That lay in his with the sun upon it.
And as the bandage knot was tightened
The two men smiled into each other's eyes.

NEW MUSIC

The lovemaking grows more intense, not less.
Ten million men and women out of work
The price of a sound currency. Tim Page
Brings us "The New, The Old, The Unexpected,"
Two hours of new music every day,
Six hours of sleep, eight of work, and art
Simmers on the back burner with desire
For Fame, for Fortune. Rules: choose one, not
    both.

The reasons for not moving grow more lame.
Ten million stories in this naked city
And one of them is ours. I'm like Tim Miller
Spraying my name in paint upon my chest,
Reminding me of who I am. A man
By any other name's a refugee.
I shall not back away, but take my stand
Where love and honesty are one, not both.

It gets more complicated with the years
And less so. There must be ten million ways
Of making love, but all I need are three:
The new, the old, the unexpected. Grace
Is like New Music hitting with the force

Of tidal waves, or like the atmosphere
So clear these mornings we forget it's how
We've always lived and breathed as one, not both.

I touch you on the eyes, and chest, and wrist.
Ten million dollars wouldn't change a thing,
The price of a sound mind. "Tim Dlugos knows,"
Voice-over from an old-time radio
Reminding me of where I used to be.
I'm here, and so are you. To make it art
Is easy when you're musical as we.
Live it or live with it: choose one, not both.

MY MAN IS FROM A
FORSTER NOVEL

Dressed to play cricket by day
Stripped to bohemian boxers at night
Late from the station
My clothing disheveled
His carriage unaltered
Smell of Monet mornings
In his starch-starched shirt
Stiff etiquette
He licks my ear
Like an Old Master
I straighten his petulant smile
With my lips
Unseen to all
His proper
Diction slips
To silent breathing
On my breast
His hands clasp the
Arc of my back like a ladder
We climb his quarters in the storm wet
While everyone is dry
I view the room where moonlight
Covers his body
In the corner of his arms

I take in everything like a colonized gift
Falling asleep
Under white pillows
A four-poster,
A Bombay nightstand
& a fan
He turns to me very naked—
An early riser
Garden sun in his eyes—
"Sit quietly beside me. Won't you
Share this view?"

PERFECTION

Late Saturday nights
after the dinner and the play or the movie
and after the first Sunday papers have come out

those late Saturday nights
when it's raining in spring or snowing in winter
and almost no cars pass by any more

on those late Saturday nights
nothing needs to be done
but the Sunday crossword

which never gets done
for its paths stretch on
deeper and deeper into the night

as word after word falls into place
but never the last word
and the mind rejoices

at how the right words can fill
this noble emptiness
and yet lead to more words

then the lamp stays lit
the night stays dark
and as long as the puzzle lasts is perfection

surely jails and asylums have opened their doors
surely no one lacks riches there is no one cast down
no one frets sleepless or cries in dreams

war and cancer can never return
there is nothing but words and the meanings
        of words
and I look up from the puzzle and tell you
        "I love you"

HAVING A COKE WITH YOU

is even more fun than going to San Sebastian, Irún,
     Hendaye, Biarritz, Bayonne
or being sick to my stomach on the Travesera de
     Gracia in Barcelona
partly because in your orange shirt you look like a
     better happier St. Sebastian
partly because of my love for you, partly because of
     your love for yoghurt
partly because of the fluorescent orange tulips
     around the birches
partly because of the secrecy our smiles take on
     before people and statuary
it is hard to believe when I'm with you that there can
     be anything as still
as solemn as unpleasantly definitive as statuary when
     right in front of it
in the warm New York 4 o'clock light we are drifting
     back and forth
between each other like a tree breathing through its
     spectacles

and the portrait show seems to have no faces in it at
     all, just paint
you suddenly wonder why in the world anyone ever
     did them

                                                    I look
at you and I would rather look at you than all the
        portraits in the world
except possibly for the *Polish Rider* occasionally and
        anyway it's in the Frick
which thank heavens you haven't gone to yet so we
        can go together the first time
and the fact that you move so beautifully more or
        less takes care of Futurism
just as at home I never think of the *Nude Descending
        a Staircase* or
at a rehearsal a single drawing of Leonardo or
        Michelangelo that used to wow me
and what good does all the research of the Impres-
        sionists do them
when they never got the right person to stand near
        the tree when the sun sank
or for that matter Marino Marini when he didn't
        pick the rider as carefully
as the horse
                    it seems they were all cheated of some
        marvellous experience
which is not going to go wasted on me which is why
        I'm telling you about it

                                32

FROM EDWARD II
(ACT I, SCENE 1)

GAVESTON (reading a letter from Edward):

"My father is deceas'd. Come, Gaveston,
And share the kingdom with thy dearest friend."
Ah, words that make me surfeit with delight!
What greater bliss can hap to Gaveston
Than live and be the favourite of a king!
Sweet prince, I come! These, these thy amorous lines
Might have enforc'd me to have swum from France,
And, like Leander, gasp'd upon the sand,
So thou wouldst smile, and take me in thine arms.
The sight of London to my exil'd eyes
Is as Elysium to a new-come soul:
Not that I love the city or the men,
But that it harbours him I hold so dear—
The king, upon whose bosom let me die,
And with the world be still at enmity.

FROM YELLOW SNOW

The lure is too strong
I want to be rich for him
I want to be famous for him,
really famous
I want him to want me for
all the wrong reasons,
for any reason
I want him to want me
until, satisfied, he
forgets all want for
anyone else,
the way that I was
never able to do.

JELAN AND JAMALI

Jelan and Jamali.
They born Lamu.
Grow together from boyness.
Grow together are one.
Together race seabirds. Share
cassava cooked in a blackened pot.

Jelan and Jamali.
Two sailors of a Lamu dhow.
Fish boat sail on water.
Jelan brown
high tones slim
long fine like rope.
Jamali is Swahili dark
warm shiny like
tanned blackness
muscles round like
knotted
rope.

Twenty-three.
Pay down on boat.
When they work they
sail.

Wazungu pay money
to ride on Jelan
and Jamali's boat.
Men women
pay to ride the waves
of Jamali and Jelan.
Jelan long fine like sisal
like rope. They love
cassava cooked in a blackened pot.

When there is no work they
sail
and race seabirds.
Smoke laugh dance on water.
Tell tales of Lamu fishermen.
Sleep on bottom of boat.
Sleep on sail as mattress.
Sleep on coils and coils
of rope.
Each dreaming in his brother's arms.
And this is an African love poem.

ANNIVERSARY SONG

Because six years have gone by since then,
because there's still nothing on earth,
nothing so sweet as a room
for two, if it's yours and mine;
because even time, that poor relation
who has seen better days,
is waving a flag for happiness today:
let's sing for joy!

And then let's get up late
like on Sunday. Let's linger
the whole morning long making love
again but better: in another way
night can't even imagine
while our room, just like time,
fills with sunlight, quiet intimacy
and the serenity of the ages.

Echo of our pleasure days,
desire, music remembered
inside the heart, so romantic
I've barely put it in my poems;
all the fragrance, unfaithful past,
what was sweet and inspires longing,

don't you see how everything you and I
once dreamed is overwhelmed by what is?

Reality—not a pretty sight—
with its awkward details of being two,
shameful nights of love without desire
and desire without love
we couldn't atone for in six centuries
of sleeping alone. And its enigmatic
shifts from betrayal to boredom,
boredom back to betrayal.

No, life's not a dream, and you know
we both tend to forget it.
But a little dreaming, that's all,
a smidgen for this occasion, hushing up
about the rest of the story, and a moment
when you and I wish each other
a long and happy life together—
I doubt it can do any harm.

TRANSLATED BY JAMES NOLAN

MY RUG MAKER FINE

For Vince King, a Navajo

slowly as I laid my head
upon his chest
the rain outside beckoned
for me to kiss him
we forgot the names that were called
and as I looked into his deep brown eyes
I saw the earth of his people
the earth of his blood
and the earth of his birth
looking at me

there was much to be said
on that rainy night
but talking came secondary
and not much was said
some names were meant to scald
they can break steadfast ties
then I heard the earth of his people
the earth of his blood
and the earth of his birth
telling me

he left on that rainy night
without a kiss

he went home forever
the rain beckoned at him to go
the earth of his people told me
he was going home
the earth of his blood called him
to come home
and the earth of his birth took him
from me

oh how my heart went on a dizzy flight
I will him miss
knowing this was going to sever
our hearts and leave a hole
I know the drum of his people
that called him home
I feel the pulse of his blood
that drew him there
I smell the scent of his birth
that made me let him go

I have endured the name
the scalding brand
I stand on my own feet now
the earth of my people

the earth of my blood
and the earth of my birth
told me to let you go
I listened
I know now
and we are free

TWO YOUNG MEN, 23 TO 24 YEARS OLD

He'd been sitting in the café since ten-thirty
expecting him to turn up any minute.
Midnight went by, and he was still waiting for him.
It was now after one-thirty, and the café was almost
    deserted.
He'd grown tired of reading newspapers
mechanically. Of his three lonely shillings
only one was left: waiting that long,
he'd spent the others on coffees and brandy.
He'd smoked all his cigarettes.
So much waiting had worn him out. Because
alone like that for so many hours,
he'd also begun to have disturbing thoughts
about the immoral life he was living.

But when he saw his friend come in—
weariness, boredom, thoughts vanished at once.

His friend brought unexpected news.
He'd won sixty pounds playing cards.

Their good looks, their exquisite youthfulness,
the sensitive love they shared
were refreshed, livened, invigorated
by the sixty pounds from the card table.

Now all joy and vitality, feeling and charm,
they went—not to the homes of their respectable
        families
(where they were no longer wanted anyway)—
they went to a familiar and very special
house of debauchery, and they asked for a bedroom
and expensive drinks, and they drank again.

And when the expensive drinks were finished
and it was close to four in the morning,
happy, they gave themselves to love.

4 A.M.

I am learning
that when he doesn't
come home he is
having a good time
and yes that is
unfaithful, but the earth so
desperately needs good times,
unfaithfulness, and water.

Arthur Rimbaud

OUR ASSHOLES ARE DIFFERENT
FROM THEIRS

Our assholes are different from theirs. I used to
    watch
Young men let down their pants behind some tree,
And in those happy floods that youth set free
I watched the architecture of our crotch.

Quite firm, in many cases pale, it owes
Its form to muscles and a wickerwork
Of hairs; for girls, the most enchanting lurk
In a dark crack where tufted satin grows.

The touching and wonderful innocence
Of painted cherubs on a Baroque shrine
Is recalled in that cheek a dimple indents . . .

Oh! If only we were naked now, and free
To watch our protruding parts align;
To whisper—both of us—in ecstasy!

TRANSLATED BY PAUL SCHMIDT

I WANT TO LOVE YOU

I want to be the door in your jamb—
always to close to your strong members.
I want to swell with our humid love
so we will be stuck together.
Love-locked, your frame around my
solid core, we'd never be jimmied apart.

I want to be your vanity drawer,
to hide my treasures in you.
I want to be the nail driven homeward
to my life-purpose by your blows.
I wish to be the foil embracing
your dark stone—together a gem.

I want to love your gold shore,
to hug, caress, and kiss your shifting contours,
to batter relentlessly against
your changeless self during my storms,
to bejewel you during high tides,
and reveal your secrets during low.

I would be a fish to spend and draw
life swimming through and breathing you.
I'd be the white to your plump yolk,

to surround and nourish you as you grow,
to help you rise if you're beaten,
to be each figure and ground for each.

. . . I want to love you . . .

Jaime Manrique

MY NIGHT WITH FEDERICO GARCÍA LORCA

(As Told by Edouard Roditi)

It happened in Paris.
Pepe asked me over to dinner
to meet a guy named Federico
who was on his way to New York.
I was nineteen years old.
Federico was eleven years older
and had just finished
a relationship in Spain
with a sculptor
who had been rotten to him.
Federico only had two lovers—
he hated promiscuous queens.

We were both Geminis.
Since astrology
was very important to him,
Federico took an interest in me.
We spoke in Spanish.
I had learned it
from my grandmother, a Sephardic
Jew, who had taught me
sixteenth-century expressions.
Federico was amused by all this.

48

We drank a lot of
wine that night.
In the morning, when I woke up,
his head lay across my nipples.
Hundreds of people
have asked me for the details:
Was Federico fabulous in bed?
I always give them my standard answer:
Federico was emotional
and vulnerable; for him
the most important thing wasn't sex
but tenderness.
I never saw him again.
The following day he left for England
then New York and Cuba.
Later, the second love
of his life was murdered
defending the Republic.

All this happened in Paris
almost sixty years ago.
It was just a night of love
but it has lasted all my life.

PAGAN SUMMER

You lay a hand on my chest.
Roll over brushing the hair of my thigh.
Tickle love sonnets on my stomach with the Chinese
     brush I gave you.
Twirl a tongue in my ear.
Lick my sleeping lips.
Guide an index finger into my asshole.
Slide your hard dick between my aching cheeks.
Three times in one night.
Too much?
But I say nothing as you push.

Our bodies clench.
We melt into a single animal.
Your grinding hipbone and my face in the pillow.
I raise my ass to meet you.
Urine rising in my throat.
Anger stifled by your moans.
Twisting our faces into obscene masks.
Your heaving body slapping the darkness in me.
Forcing me down into the green grass of summer.
The cool blades stinging my lips.
Stabbing me in the nose.
Hands liver-spotted.
That familiar face.

White wreath of hair crowning a bald head.
Suit jacket hiding a gothic whiteness. Those flabby
    thighs.
Too much for a child of seven.
But oh god I say nothing as you push and push and
    push.

MAKING LOVE TO MYSELF

When I do it, I remember how it was with us.
Then my hands remember too,
and you're with me again, just the way it was.

After work when you'd come in and
turn the TV off and sit on the edge of the bed,
filling the room with gasoline smell from your
    overalls,
trying not to wake me which you always did.
I'd breathe out long and say,
"Hi Jess, you tired baby?"
You'd say not so bad and rub my belly,
not after me really, just being sweet,
and I always thought I'd die a little
because you smelt like burnt leaves or woodsmoke.

We were poor as Job's turkey but we lived well—
the food, a few good movies, good dope, lots of talk,
lots of you and me trying on each other's skin.

What a sweet gift this is,
done with my memory, my cock and hands.

Sometimes I'd wake up wondering if I should fix
coffee for us before work,
almost thinking you're here again, almost seeing
your work jacket on the chair.

I wonder if you remember what
we promised when you took the job in Laramie?
Our way of staying with each other.
We promised there'd always be times
when the sky was perfectly lucid,
that we could remember each other through that.
You could remember me at my worktable
or in the all-night diners,
though we'd never call or write.

I just have to stop here Jess.
I just have to stop.

Michael Lassell

BRADY STREET, SAN FRANCISCO

For Roberto Muñoz

The apartment
is still standing, still about to fall.
It's circled now in Technicolors of
competing graffiti
more artful than we were to
stay in love.
Our names in cement are long gone.
It's my first time back since the news.

From the street
nothing seems to have changed.
My mind too has trapped the action in mid-flight:
how I hid in the closet (naked) the
first morning your family descended unannounced
and told your father we'd had
balls for breakfast when my Spanish slipped on
eggs. You shot your
one-note nasal laugh and spun on your heel,
but I'd cracked the shell of tension.
Your mother sat on the couch—
a miniature goddess of plenty, her feet
not touching the floor—and adopted me
in her knowing smile.

Here's a junk drawer more of memories:
an orange cat that lived through an air-shaft fall;
the Twin Peaks fog from our bedroom window bay;
snacking on Stevie Wonder and your skin;
the double mattress we had to carry home
on our backs because
it cost every cent we'd saved.

After the first fight over nothing you
slammed into the street. I screamed
from the third floor into the dark I'd
die if
you didn't love me; you cried and
crept back up the stairs creak by
indolent creak.
We stayed together.
That time.
And when the loving was over—
three years, two apartments,
and a continent later—
no one died. Not
altogether. At least not
right away.

We left behind the odor of queers in the carpet,
the grease from our last
cooked meal,
a hole I punched in the plaster with my anger
and covered with the Desiderata so
the landlord wouldn't howl.

You see, it only takes a score of years
to make the bitter memories sweet,
like lemons in a sugar glaze.
I'd eat an orchard of them for you now
if you could be alive again to see me try.

OFFERTORY ON A SEVENTH ANNIVERSARY

on this day
when there's no holiness
in all this madness of tests
where the heart is
with the sharpest brass knife
let us carve a tiny star
on each other's chest
watch them light up
bright red
we will bless them with our lips
drink life
neither a seven-year itch
nor death
can split

HERE

everything extraneous has burned away
this is how burning feels in the fall
of the final year not like leaves in a blue
October but as if the skin were a paper lantern
full of trapped moths beating their fired wings
and yet I can lie on this hill just above you
a foot beside where I will lie myself
soon soon and for all the wrack and blubber
feel still how we were warriors when the
merest morning sun in the garden was a
kingdom after Room 1010 war is not all
death it turns out war is what little
thing you hold on to refugeed and far from home
oh sweetie will you please forgive me this
that every time I opened a box of anything
Glad Bags One-A-Days KINGSIZE was
the worst I'd think will you still be here
when the box is empty Rog Rog who will
play boy with me now that I bucket with tears
through it all when I'd cling beside you sobbing
you'd shrug it off with the quietest *I'm still
here* I have your watch in the top drawer
which I don't dare wear yet help me please
the boxes grocery home day after day
the junk that keeps men spotless but it doesn't

matter now how long they last or I
the day has taken you with it and all
there is now is burning dark the only green
is up by the grave and this little thing
of telling the hill I'm here oh I'm here

THE DEATH OF ANTINOÜS

When the beautiful young man drowned—
accidentally, swimming at dawn
in a current too swift for him,
or obedient to some cult
of total immersion that promised
the bather would come up divine,

mortality rinsed from him—
Hadrian placed his image everywhere,
a marble Antinoüs staring across
the public squares where a few dogs
always scuffled, planted
in every squalid little crossroad

at the farthest corners of the Empire.
What do we want in any body
but the world? And if the lover's
inimitable form was nowhere,
then he would find it everywhere,
though the boy became simply more dead

as the sculptors embodied him.
Wherever Hadrian might travel,
the beloved figure would be there

first: the turn of his shoulders,
the exact marble nipples,
the drowned face not really lost

to the Nile—which has no appetite,
merely takes in anything
without judgment or expectation—
but lost into its own multiplication,
an artifice rubbed with oils and acid
so that the skin might shine.

Which of these did I love?
Here is his hair, here his hair
again. Here the chiseled liquid waist
I hold because I cannot hold it.
If only one of you, he might have said
to any of the thousand marble boys anywhere,

would speak. Or the statues might have been enough,
the drowned boy blurred as much by memory
as by water, molded toward an essential,
remote ideal. Longing, of course,
becomes its own object, the way
that desire can make anything into a god.

David Bergman

A DREAM OF NIGHTINGALES

In Memory of Jerry Thompson

The Friday before your funeral I taught
Keats to my sophomore class. Little did they care
for the truth of beauty or the grace of truth,
but his being "half in love with easeful death"
penetrated through the smugness of their youth,
and I thought of you drawing me to the rear
window one early spring to hear in rapture
a bird hidden among the flowering pear.

You held your cat tight so that he could not scare
off such music as hadn't been heard all winter.
When you flew South to escape the arctic blast
and home again heard that dark-winged creature
    sing,
tell me, did he then reveal himself at last
as you believed he'd be—pure and beckoning?

Paul Goodman

LONG LINES: YOUTH AND AGE

Like a hot stone your cock weighs on mine,
     young man,
and your face has become brutish and congested.
I'd draw back and gaze at it but drunk with carbon
     dioxide
we cannot stop snuffling each other's breath.

I am surprised you lust for a grayhead like me
and what a waste for me to grapple so much pleasure
with sliding palms holding your thin body
firmly while you squirm, till it is time to come.

Come, lad . . . I have come with him for company
to his pounding heart. We are wet. Wistfully
I play with his black hair while he falls asleep
minute by minute, slowly, unlike my restless life.

It is quiet on his little boat. "He's a noisy lover,"
I notice idly—the April air is keen—
"but he has no human speech." It's I who say
the words like "I love you" or "Thank you."

BREAKFAST

I am sitting here at my desk in the morning as usual
with the tie-rack on the wall in front of me.
(L., which stands for love, is in the other room
writing his novel near the plants.)
My favorite green tie
that always makes my eyes luminous when I wear it
had its tail cut off by L.
because he said it grew too long.
His shoes always loosen, and his pants stretch;
he changes the size of everything, like he did my life.
He makes all things grow, I will testify to that.

I am good with plants however:
Where I love it is green.
Where L. loves
it grows like nebulae, larger and larger:
He gets bigger and bigger in my arms
like a Picasso nude that smacks you in the face
        with a tit
while the goodies of her body are breaking out
        all over,
her legs writhing in ecstasy: she is titled
        BREAKFAST.
And you look at all this,
it is absolute Heaven and you have it in your arms;

so you start kissing like mad just to hold it down,
and you find to your surprise that you didn't take off
    into space
but you sank deliciously into a sea of luminous
    green,
into a garden you never grew, a garden that God gave
    you—
and you've got such a hard-on for this delightful
    youth
like you never knew was possible.

Thom Gunn

THE HUG

It was your birthday, we had drunk and dined
  Half of the night with our old friend
    Who'd showed us in the end
  To a bed I reached in one drunk stride.
    Already I lay snug,
And drowsy with the wine dozed on one side.

I dozed, I slept. My sleep broke on a hug,
  Suddenly, from behind,
In which the full lengths of our bodies pressed:
  Your instep to my heel,
  My shoulder-blades against your chest.
  It was not sex, but I could feel
  The whole strength of your body set,
    Or braced, to mine,
    And locking me to you
  As if we were still twenty-two
  When our grand passion had not yet
    Become familial.
  My quick sleep had deleted all
  Of intervening time and place.
    I only knew
The stay of your secure firm dry embrace.

SONNET 90

I'm much dearer to myself than I used to be;
since I've gotten you in my heart, I value myself
    more,
as a stone to which carving has been added
is worth more than its original rock.
    Or, as a written or painted page or sheet
is better thought of than any scrap or shred,
so do I of myself, since I became
a target marked by your face, which does not
    hurt me.
    Secure with such a mark, I go anywhere
like one who has with him amulets or weapons
that make every danger fade away from him.
    I prevail against water and against fire,
with your mark I restore light to all the blind,
and with my spittle I can cure every poison.

TRANSLATED BY JAMES M. SASLOW

LOVE POEM

At 4:30 A.M., I wake up
from a nightmare, bump
through the dark apartment
to pee, then sit and smoke
a cigarette in the living
room. When I get back
in bed, Ira wakes up
and says: "You're a sweet
man, do you know that?"
I tell him I've been having
bad dreams. I'm lying on
my back; he tells me to roll
on my side. As I do, he presses
against me from behind and
wraps his arm around my chest.
"You're safe now," he whispers
into my neck. "Go back to sleep.
You won't have any more bad dreams."

FRANCISCO X. ALARCÓN (b. 1954) is the author of nine volumes of poetry, including *Body in Flames/Cuerpo en llamas* (1990) and *Snake Poems: An Aztec Invocation* (1992), both published by Chronicle Books. One of the few openly gay Chicano male writers in the U.S., he is the recipient of numerous awards, including the American Book Award.

JACK ANDERSON (b. 1935) is the author of eight books of poetry. He is also a dance critic for *The New York Times* and *The Dancing Times* of London and the author of six books on dance history and criticism.

W. H. AUDEN (1907–73) has been called the first authentically modern poet writing in English. One of the most influential British modernists, he was a key figure in the circle that included fellow literary travelers Christopher Isherwood and Stephen Spender.

RICHARD BARNFIELD (1574–1627) was the author of *The Affectionate Shepherd* (1594), *Cynthia* (published with twenty sonnets in 1595), a satire entitled *Lady Pecunia* (1598), and a series of homoerotic pastoral poems about Daphnis's love for Ganymede.

DAVID BERGMAN (b. 1950) won the George Elliston Prize for Poetry for *Cracking the Code* (Ohio State University Press, 1985). His latest book of poetry is *The*

Care and Treatment of Pain (Kairos Editions, 1994). He is the editor of *The Violet Quill Reader* (St. Martin's Press, 1994) and *Men on Men 5* (Plume, 1994).

WALTA BORAWSKI (1947–94) was the author of *Sexually Dangerous Poet* (Good Gay Poets, 1984) and *Lingering in a Silk Shirt* (Fag Rag Books, 1994). His poems have been anthologized in *Son of the Male Muse* (The Crossing Press, 1983), *Gay & Lesbian Poetry in Our Time* (St. Martin's Press, 1988), and *Poets for Life* (Crown Publishers, 1989). He died of complications from AIDS on 9 February 1994.

REGIE CABICO (b. 1970) is a member of the Writers' Community at The Writer's Voice. His poetry and criticism have appeared in *Ikon, Cocodrilo, Java Journal, The St. Mark's Poetry Project*, and *Aloud: Voices from the Nuyorican Poets Cafe* (Henry Holt, 1994). He is the winner of the 1993 New York Poetry Slam.

GAIUS VALERIUS CATULLUS (84–54 B.C.) was among the great lyric poets of ancient Rome. His two great love affairs, recorded in his poetry, were with Lesbia and the youth Iuventius.

CONSTANTINE P. CAVAFY (1863–1933), Greek by blood and Egyptian by birth, is widely considered the most significant Greek poet of the twentieth century. The unapologetic inclusion of his homosexuality in his poems makes him one of the most important forefathers of modern gay poetry.

DENNIS COOPER (b. 1953) is the author of the novels *Closer* (1989), *Frisk* (1991), *Try* (1994), and a collection of stories, *Wrong* (1989), all published by Grove Press. His poetry collections include *Idols* (The SeaHorse Press, 1979), *The Tenderness of the Wolves* (The Crossing Press, 1982), and *He Cried* (Black Star, 1984). In 1995, Grove will publish his selected poems.

HART CRANE (1899–1932), perhaps the unhappiest gay poet of the century, was born in Ohio. Alcoholic and argumentative, he traveled widely, settled in New York, and published his first book at twenty-seven, the second (and last), *The Bridge,* at thirty. Three years later, he jumped from a steamer in the Gulf of Mexico and drowned.

GAVIN GEOFFREY DILLARD (b. 1954) is an artist, poet, songwriter, and, in his own word, pornographer. He is the author of eight collections of poetry, including *Waiting for the Virgin* (The SeaHorse Press, 1985) and *The Naked Poet* (Bhakti Books, 1989).

TIM DLUGOS (1950–90) was a longtime contributing editor of *Christopher Street.* His books include *Entre Nous* (Little Caesar Press, 1982) and *Strong Place* (Amethyst Press, 1992). He died of AIDS in December of 1990.

MARK DOTY (b. 1953) won the National Book Critics Circle Award and the *Los Angeles Times* Book Prize for his most recent book, *My Alexandria* (University of Illinois Press, 1993). A recent Guggenheim Fellow, he lives in Provincetown, Massachusetts.

EDWARD FIELD (b. 1924) won a Lambda Literary Award for his most recent book, *Counting Myself Lucky: Selected*

Poems 1963–1992 (Black Sparrow Press, 1992). He lives in Greenwich Village, New York.

KENNY FRIES (b. 1960) received a Gregory Kolovakos Award for AIDS Writing for *The Healing Notebooks* (Open Books, 1990). *Anesthesia,* a new book, is forthcoming. His play, *A Human Equation,* premiered at La Mama E.T.C. in New York City, and his poems have appeared in publications such as *The American Voice, The James White Review,* and *The Kenyon Review.*

BEN GEBOE (b. 1965) is also known as Ben the Dancer. A Yankton Sioux, he grew up on the Rosebud Sioux Reservation in South Dakota and is a cofounder of We Wah and Bar Chee Ampe, Twospirits in New York City.

JAIME GIL DE BIEDMA (1929–90) was born in Barcelona just before the Spanish Civil War. One of the most influential poets of postwar Spain, he became a legendary figure in the long struggle of his country to emerge from the fascist dictatorship of Francisco Franco. He died of AIDS in 1990.

JOHN GILL (b. 1924) is copublisher of The Crossing Press in Freedom, California. He has published six volumes of poetry. *From the Diary of Peter Doyle* (Alembic Press, 1982) and *Between Worlds: New and Selected Poems* (Hanging Loose Press, 1993) are his most recent titles. There is a volume of his collected poems in the works.

ALLEN GINSBERG (b. 1926) is doubtlessly the best known poet living in America. A founder of the Beat movement, and longtime resident of Greenwich Village,

Ginsberg has been a central fixture of arts and letters since the publication of *Howl and Other Poems* (City Lights Books, 1956).

PAUL GOODMAN (1911–72) was known primarily as a psychologist and seminal social critic. Highly regarded for *Growing Up Absurd* (Vintage Books, 1960), Goodman was also a noted poet and writer of fiction.

THOM GUNN (b. 1929), English-born, has lived in California since 1954, currently in San Francisco. His recent books include *The Man with Night Sweats* (1992) and *Collected Poems* (1994), both published by Farrar, Straus, and Giroux, and *Shelf Life* (University of Michigan Press, 1994), a collection of essays.

ESSEX HEMPHILL (b. 1957) is the editor of the award-winning anthology *Brother to Brother: New Writings by Black Gay Men* (Alyson Publications, 1991) and the author of *Ceremonies* (Plume, 1992), an award-winning collection of prose and poetry. His poetry is featured in two groundbreaking black gay video and film documents, *Tongues Untied* by the late Marlon Riggs and *Looking for Langston* by Isaac Julien.

A. E. HOUSMAN (1859–1936) failed his Oxford final examinations because of his unrequited love for a fellow student. He nonetheless became a brilliant classicist and professor of Latin (at Cambridge). He is best known for *A Shropshire Lad* (1896). Its themes of fleeting beauty and tragic, early death seem sadly modern in 1994.

GRAHAM JACKSON (b. 1949) is the Toronto-born and -raised author of a book of Japanese-inspired poems, four collections of short fiction, a critical survey of Canadian dance, and a two-volume study of male-male intimacy. He practices as a Jungian analyst in his hometown.

CARY ALAN JOHNSON (b. 1960) is an author, Africanist, and human rights activist. Originally from Brooklyn, Johnson has lived and traveled throughout Africa, Europe, and North America. His poetry has appeared in *The Road Before Us* (Galiens Press, 1991) and *Here to Dare* (Galiens Press, 1992).

EDMUND KEELEY (b. 1928; cotranslator, C. P. Cavafy) is professor of English and creative writing at Princeton University, director of the Hellenic Studies Program, and the author of five novels.

MICHAEL LASSELL (b. 1947) is the author of *Poems for Lost and Un-lost Boys* (Amelia, 1985), the Lambda Literary Award–winning *Decade Dance* (Alyson Publications, 1990), and *The Hard Way* (Richard Kasak Books, 1994), a collection of poetry and prose. His writing has appeared in *Men on Men 3* (Dutton, 1990), *High Risk* (Dutton, 1991), *New Worlds of Literature* (W. W. Norton & Company, 1994), and *Friends and Lovers* (Dutton, 1995).

DAVID LEVINSON (b. 1969), originally from San Antonio, Texas, graduated from Columbia University in New York City. He has studied poetry with David Trinidad, and his work appeared in *5 x 7,* a chapbook published by Beth Fein, a member of Trinidad's workshop. His poetry was selected by special editor Kenny Fries for inclusion in *The James White Review*. He lives in Brooklyn.

TIMOTHY LIU (b. 1965) received the 1992 Norma Farber First Book Award for his book of poems, *Vox Angelica* (alicejamesbooks, 1992). New work is forthcoming in *The Kenyon Review, The Paris Review,* and *The Quarterly.*

JAIME MANRIQUE (b. 1949) received the National Poetry Award of his native Colombia for his first volume of poetry. His most recent novel is *Latin Moon in Manhattan* (St. Martin's Press, 1992). He has just completed a young adult biography of Federico García Lorca.

CHRISTOPHER MARLOWE (1564–93) coined the phrase "Who loves not boys and tobacco is a fool." A flamboyant and controversial character rumored to be a secret agent, he was killed in a tavern brawl after writing such plays as *Dr. Faustus, The Jew of Malta,* and *Edward II* and before completing the long narrative poem, "Hero and Leander."

MARCUS VALERIUS MARTIALIS (*c.* A.D. 40–104) was born in Spain and became one of the outstanding Latin poets of the Roman Empire. His verses served as models for the modern epigram.

MICHELANGELO (1475–1564), a towering figure of the Italian Renaissance, and painter of the Sistine Chapel, based much of his poetry, as well as his sculptures, on his young male lovers.

PAUL MONETTE (b. 1945) won the National Book Award in 1992 for his memoir, *Becoming a Man: Half a Life Story* (Harcourt Brace Jovanovich, 1992). He is the author of numerous novels, screenplays, collections of poetry, and the autobiographical *Borrowed Time* (Harcourt

Brace Jovanovich, 1988). *West of Yesterday, East of Summer* (St. Martin's Press), a volume of new and selected poems, appeared in 1994.

JAMES NOLAN (b. 1949; translator, Jaime Gil de Biedma) is the author of *Why I Live in the Forest* (Wesleyan University Press, 1974) and *What Moves Is Not the Wind* (Wesleyan University Press, 1980); and the translator of Pablo Neruda's *Stones of the Sky* (Copper Canyon Press, 1987).

EUGENE O'CONNOR (b. 1948; translator, Catullus and Martial), currently an editor at Prometheus Books in Buffalo, New York, has taught classics at the University of California, the College of Wooster, and the University of Montana. His chief scholarly interests are classical and neo-Latin satire and epigram.

FRANK O'HARA (1926–66) was born in Baltimore, grew up in Massachusetts, graduated from Harvard, and worked at the Museum of Modern Art in New York City. After five well-regarded books, he was killed by a sanitation vehicle while asleep on the beach at Fire Island at the age of forty.

CHARLES L. ORTLEB (b. 1950) is the publisher of *Christopher Street, Stonewall News, New York Native, Theater-Week,* and *Opera Monthly.*

ROBERT PETERS (b. 1924) is an indefatigable poet, critic, playwright, fiction writer, actor, and teacher whose books include *What Dillinger Meant to Me* (The Sea-Horse Press, 1983) and *Poems: Selected and New, 1967–1991* (Asylum Arts, 1992). He lives in California with his lover of twenty-five years, poet and novelist Paul Trachtenberg.

CRAIG A. REYNOLDS (1952–94) was a native of Washington, D.C. His poetry appeared in numerous journals and anthologies, including *The Road Before Us: 100 Gay Black Poets* (Galiens Press, 1991) and *Here to Dare: 10 Gay Black Poets* (Galiens Press, 1992). He died of cancer shortly before this book went to press.

ARTHUR RIMBAUD (1854–91) was notorious in his day for his adolescent affair with poet Paul Verlaine, ten years his senior. After writing several scandalously scatological poems with his young lover, Verlaine spent two years in jail for shooting him. Rimbaud stopped writing poetry at age nineteen.

ASSOTTO SAINT (né Yves François Lubin, 1957–94), poet, dramatist, and composer, was the author of *Stations* (1989) and the posthumous *Wishing for Wings* (1994), both of them published by his own company, Galiens Press, which also published *The Road Before Us* (1991) and *Here to Dare* (1992). He died of AIDS on 29 June 1994.

JAMES M. SASLOW (b. 1947; translator, Michelangelo) is the author of *Ganymede in the Renaissance: Homosexuality in Art and Society* (Yale University Press, 1986). A former New York editor of *The Advocate,* he is a contributor to *Long Road to Freedom: The Advocate History of the Gay and Lesbian Movement* (St. Martin's Press, 1994).

PAUL SCHMIDT (b. 1934; translator, Arthur Rimbaud) is widely known as a translator from Latin, Greek, French, German, and Russian. He has translated the collected work of Rimbaud and of Velimir Khlebnikov, as well as plays by Molière, Chekhov, Brecht, and Genet.

WILLIAM SHAKESPEARE (1564–1616) is, arguably, the greatest writer who ever lived. Many of his stunningly romantic 154 sonnets were written for a young man of aristocratic birth. His three dozen plays, performed in his lifetime exclusively by men and boys, introduced to English literature a fascination with androgyny and the comic eroticism of mistaken sexual identity (particularly when involving twins).

PHILIP SHERRARD (b. 1922; cotranslator, C. P. Cavafy) is the well-known author of a number of books on modern Greek religion and culture.

DAVID TRINIDAD (b. 1953) is widely regarded as among the finest gay poets of his generation. His books include *Answer Song* (High Risk/Serpent's Tail, 1994) and *Hand Over Heart: Poems 1981–1988* (Amethyst Press, 1991). He lives in New York City.

JAMES L. WHITE (1936–81) was trained as a classical ballet dancer. After a successful dance career, he wrote four books of poetry, including *The Salt Ecstasies* (Graywolf Press, 1982). Devoted to Native American culture, White edited two books of contemporary Native American poetry.

WALT WHITMAN (1819–92) wrote only one book of poetry in his life, the monumental *Leaves of Grass,* which he enlarged and revised through nine editions, establishing modern American poetry in the process. Not only the most important poet in American literary history, he is, without question, the father, mother, and soul of gay writing in America.

BIL WRIGHT (b. 1957) is a playwright, fiction writer, poet, and director. His work has appeared in *Men on Men 3* (Dutton, 1990), *The Road Before Us* (Galiens Press, 1991), the play anthology *Tough Acts to Follow* (Alamo Square Press, 1992), and many other publications. A 1994 artist-in-residence with the Mabou Mines Theater Company, he received a 1993 Playwright's Award from La Mama E.T.C.

Index of First Lines